T0272983

50 BOOKS TO
READ IF YOU'RE...
A HOPELESS
ROMANTIC

ERIC KARL ANDERSON

murdoch books

Sydney | London

LOVE IS THE ANSWER

What makes a love story truly swoon worthy? Many involve sympathetic heroines or heroes, an alluring stranger and a rendezvous filled with anticipation. However, great romances aren't only about the meet-cute where a chance encounter leads two individuals to gaze upon one another. They also involve challenges which may prevent the couple from being together. Many romances are impeded by historical or social conflicts, disapproving families, rival suitors or personal uncertainty about whether the other person is truly *the one*. This is the emotional tension which keeps us wrapped up in the tale hoping they'll beat the odds and find their happy ending. If you love a captivating romance as much as I do, here are fifty suggestions for books with amorous stories.

Some of these books are classics, with couples who have permeated popular culture, from Cathy and Heathcliff to Elizabeth and Mr Darcy. There are more modern tales whose pairings have expressed the romantic plight of a newer generation, from Marianne and Connell to Elio and Oliver. I've also suggested a number of lesser-known books which would complement these established stories and offer surprising variations on familiar tropes. Many include pioneering couples who defy the limitations of their situation and whose passion transcends time. In doing so they can give a fresh view of the past and a renewed understanding of the power of love.

Of course, not every romance ends happily. There is a lot of longing, heartache and tragedy in these stories as well. Circumstances can tear couples apart who would otherwise spend the rest of their days in bliss. Individuals might pursue unhealthy relationships or not even understand what they truly desire. But even if the stars don't align for all these pairings, there remains the possibility of what might have been. For some, a fleeting moment can fill a heart for a lifetime.

Every love story is unique. From feverish flings to forbidden encounters to devoted partners, passion can be found in the most unlikely of places. Nostalgia is a powerful part of every relationship so all of these tales are worth revisiting to experience again that first warm glance or tentative kiss. These titles approach romance in all its beautiful forms. Delve in and be prepared to fall in love again.

NB The publication dates throughout apply to the year of first publication in the country of origin. Where several translations of a book exist, I have selected the one I'm most familiar with.

DAVID NICHOLLS * 2009

Is there one person who you've known for many years that – if circumstances were different – might have been *the one*? Emma and Dexter form a bond and friendship on their graduation night during which they speculate about what their lives will be like when they are forty. Throughout the novel we follow their many successes and failures by checking in with them on this same day of the year for the next twenty years. There's a persistent romantic tension which is complicated by their aspirations and different relationships. However, as we catch up with them through the years, each seemingly ordinary day might be the one on which there is a pivotal change that will bring these two together or tear them apart forever. This is the ultimate novel about youthful expectations versus the hard realities of adulthood. It also meaningfully depicts larger social changes throughout the 1980s and '90s.

David Nicholls began his career as an actor and screen writer, but this novel became his breakout bestseller which was adapted into a film in 2011. Superficial comparisons could easily be made between this book and *When Harry Met Sally*, but this story is wholly unique and utterly absorbing.

WUTHERING HEIGHTS

EMILY BRONTË

1847

Out on the windy moors we encounter the legend of Cathy and Heathcliff before actually meeting them on the page. This is a love affair so energetic and stormy that when the unassuming Mr Lockwood becomes snowbound in the remote farmhouse of Wuthering Heights, the ghost of Cathy comes pounding on his window. As the story unfolds we learn how this couple grew to both love and hate one another. In addition, the fallout of their relationship substantially affects the next generation and feeds into Heathcliff's vengeful scheme. This is a story in which the romantic and Gothic mix to chronicle a passionate affair wracked by class conflict and psychological torment.

Some consider this nineteenth-century novel to be more of an anti-romance as it contains so much hatefulness. Perhaps your perspective on this issue depends on your age when you read the book. While a younger reader might respond to the conflicted passion and intense longing, an adult might focus on the darkly disturbing nature of the characters. No matter how you feel about this couple, having inspired many film and stage adaptations, they are eternally locked together in their epically tempestuous relationship.

BRIDGET JONES'S DIARY

HELEN FIELDING * 1996

Just as bibliophiles obsessively make lists about books, Bridget Jones diligently records her daily weight, calorie intake and number of cigarettes smoked. This eminently witty novel presents the journals of a thirty-something woman living and working in London. She's fearful of dying alone, but is torn between two relationships. Will she choose her dashing boss Daniel Cleaver who is also a womaniser? Or her former childhood friend Mark Darcy who is now an uptight barrister? The tension of this love triangle is played out against the backdrop of Bridget's sympathetic struggles as a city career woman. Her tale encapsulates the uneven quest for self-improvement while fending off misogynists and megalo-maniacs. The tension between self-image and the reality of how we are is amplified in the new-media age which Bridget inhabits. The story strikes a chord with anyone who is plied by family and friends with the question, 'How's your love life?'

Helen Fielding was inspired to write a modernised version of Jane Austen's *Pride and Prejudice* in a series of newspaper columns about Bridget's life. These articles were eventually formed into this book, which also inspired numerous sequels as well as a series of films starring Renée Zellweger.

THE TIME TRAVELER'S WIFE

AUDREY NIFFENEGGER

2003

Many great romances begin with a chance encounter, but what if you knew the time and place you were going to meet the love of your life? When artist Claire meets Henry at the Newberry Library in 1991, it's the first time he sees her, but Claire has received visits from Henry since she was a girl. That's because Henry has a rare genetic disorder called chrono-impairment, which causes him to involuntarily travel through time. Needless to say, this causes a lot of unique issues in their relationship. Not only does Henry frequently disappear, but also there are dangers associated with his appearing in unexpected places. Claire is often left pining while Henry acquires surprising knowledge about the past and the future. This unique combination of science fiction and romance was partly inspired by Homer's *Odyssey*. It raises questions about the impact time has on relationships and shows how transience and loss are part of any love story.

This debut became an award-winning bestseller that has been adapted into a film, TV series and stage musical. Although Niffenegger stated in 2013 that she was working on a sequel, at the time of writing this, it has still not been published and fans can only hope that it will appear soon.

NORMAL PEOPLE

SALLY ROONEY * 2018

Every generation needs a great new love story and this novel dynamically captures the feeling of modern life from the past decade. Marianne and Connell come from very different socio-economic backgrounds in rural Ireland. Connell's mother works as a cleaner at Marianne's upscale family home. The differences in class seem inconsequential at first, but as they get older it has more of an effect on how they connect to each other. The story charts the staggered journey of their bond from 2011 to 2015 as their passion is sometimes stymied by circumstance and tragic misunderstanding. Like an updated Jane Austen novel, Rooney's story takes seriously the struggle to find a real emotional connection amid societal influences. It shows the effect that social perception, wealth, power and emotional baggage have upon the couple's friendship and romance. But these issues linger in the background without intruding upon the pleasures to be found in the plot as we wonder: will they or won't they get together?

Rooney has a talent for writing about the emotional core and inner conflicts of her characters without elaborate language. This bestseller was turned into a popular BBC TV series, which only intensified what critics call 'Sally Rooney fever'.

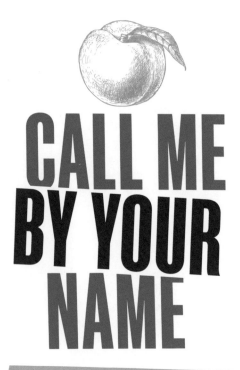

CALL ME BY YOUR NAME

ANDRÉ ACIMAN * 2007

This is one of the ultimate teenage summer romances. Precocious seventeen-year-old Elio lives with his parents in Italy. They invite twenty-four-year-old grad student Oliver to stay with them as a house guest for six weeks. Elio's strong attraction towards Oliver gradually develops into tender feelings and leads to a series of sexual encounters. Though Elio is bisexual and continues to date a local girl, he's powerfully drawn to this older man. Not only is there a physical connection, but they have many meaningful discussions about life and art. It's an affair Elio will never forget. Filled with the heat of Italian sunshine, confidential exchanges, simmering sexual tension and dream-clouded musings, this story is utterly immersive and emotionally powerful. After reading this novel you'll never look at a peach in the same way again.

This beloved tale was turned into a 2017 film starring Armie Hammer and Timothée Chalamet which captured the hearts of a generation and attracted a large international fanbase. Interestingly, it was watching the film which inspired André Aciman to revisit his characters in the sequel *Find Me*, which was published in 2019.

THE
WELL OF
LONELINESS

RADCLYFFE HALL * 1928

Stephen Gordon is born to an upper-class English family and gets stuck with a boy's name because her father wanted a son. However, as she gets older, Stephen finds she's also naturally drawn to wearing more masculine clothing and develops crushes on women. Her frustrated longing can never be fulfilled in a satisfying way because she doesn't know how to label herself and her desires are scorned by those around her. Over the course of the novel, Stephen discovers the words with which to describe herself and this leads to her liberation. Though she establishes a mutually loving relationship with another woman and meets groups of like-minded people in Paris, she's frustrated that she isn't accepted by larger society. This is a powerfully political novel of deep passion whose tragic elements are tempered by humour and warm-hearted feelings.

Though this novel was banned after its initial publication and wasn't made publicly available in Britain again until 1949, it has since been acknowledged as a pioneering classic and a lesbian story which sympathetically portrays the struggle of its protagonist as she seeks to understand herself, join a like-minded community and find a loving partner.

REBECCA

DAPHNE DU MAURIER

1938

Little does the naive and unnamed narrator of this novel realise that when she marries the wealthy widower Maxim de Winter, she's really entering into a love triangle with a ghost. Becoming the mistress of the beautiful estate of Manderley may seem like a dream but she's constantly made aware that the late Rebecca was the first Mrs de Winter. Any attempts she makes to impress the household pale in comparison to the glamorous Rebecca. Even the intimidatingly cold housekeeper Mrs Danvers still remains loyal to her former mistress. A dark mystery lies behind Rebecca's death and, as the truth gradually comes to the surface, so does an ever-changing portrait of this vivacious personality who was both loved and scorned. We may never get Rebecca's point of view but her presence fills this highly atmospheric and enthralling Gothic tale.

This great classic has remained in print ever since it was first published. It was so successful that du Maurier adapted it for the stage and it was soon turned into a film by Alfred Hitchcock. In fact, the film director clearly had an affinity for this author's gripping psychodramas as he also made films of *Jamaica Inn* and *The Birds*.

AMERICANAH

CHIMAMANDA NGOZI ADICHIE * 2013

Can a teenage romance survive a fifteen-year separation? Though Ifemelu and Obinze fall in love in their Nigerian secondary school, they find it necessary to leave the country as it's under a military dictatorship. While they are split apart by an ocean, Ifemelu discovers there are different forms of racial distinctions in America and writes a popular blog concerning her thoughts on this subject. Meanwhile, Obinze experiences what it means to be an undocumented immigrant working in England before he becomes a successful businessman. Though many years later they are reunited in a newly democratic Nigeria, their experiences have permanently changed them. They must renegotiate their relationship and decide whether they are meant to be together. This is a story filled with insightful cultural observations and it evokes a couple's unique romantic dynamic in such a moving way. It shows how love can be affected by obligations, circumstance and individual pride.

Adichie is an engaging and award-winning writer of fiction, but also a powerful social commentator, having written many influential pieces on feminism, nationality, grief and race. She makes us challenge our assumptions about the world.

THE MERMAID OF BLACK CONCH

MONIQUE ROFFEY

2020

There have been many tales of mermaids falling in love with land-dwelling men, but never one like this. In fact, there are three different romances which take place on the fictional Caribbean island in this novel. A Rastafarian fisherman falls in love with a cursed mermaid; after a ten-year separation a white proprietor is reunited with the Black man she fell in love with in her youth; and the local female gossipmonger seduces a corrupt cop to draw him into her troublemaking scheme.

Their tales are dramatised to give a dynamic portrait of love when it's impacted by time, greed, race and colonialism. But at the centre of this novel is the fantastical story of Aycayia, an indigenous woman who was cursed by the women in the village long ago because she was perceived to be a beautiful threat. For centuries she has lived a lonely existence in the ocean as a mermaid. Now, just when she has found new love, a hurricane is brewing that threatens to upturn the whole island. This romance playfully engages with folklore and legends to tell a uniquely seductive tale.

Roffey's writing is highly evocative and this imaginative novel won the coveted Costa Book of the Year Award.

BROOKLYN

COLM TÓIBÍN * 2009

Not only must the young heroine of this novel choose between two men, but she must choose between two countries. Eilis Lacey comes of age in 1950s Ireland, but as there is little opportunity for employment, she seizes an opportunity to live and work in America. There she establishes a life for herself in vibrant New York City and falls for an Italian plumber. However, when she's called back to Ireland because of a death in the family, she is reunited with an Irish man who seems to be her perfect match. Tóibín atmospherically evokes the landscapes of two very different places that are in the process of radical social and political change. This is a tale of migration and the process of maturity which forces the characters to make crucial choices that will affect the rest of their lives. The heartrending dilemma at the centre of this novel grips us until the end.

Tóibín is one of Ireland's leading writers. This novel was nominated for multiple awards and was ranked amongst the *Guardian*'s list of the 100 best books of the twenty-first century. It was also turned into a feature film with a script written by Nick Hornby and starring Saoirse Ronan.

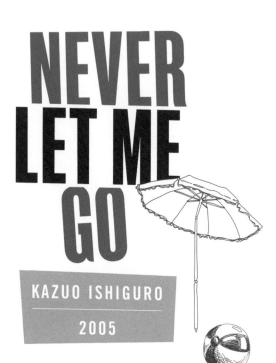

NEVER LET ME GO

KAZUO ISHIGURO

2005

DATE READ

At first this novel appears to simply be about a delicately balanced love triangle taking place at an English boarding school. But things quickly turn sinister when students Kathy, Ruth and Tommy learn that they have been raised for a specific purpose which will drastically reduce their lifespan. The way this knowledge and the events which follow impact their choices and their relationship is heart-wrenching. There's also much more lurking beneath the surface of this story even after its shocking secret has been revealed. Kathy describes her experiences and memories in a breathtaking way which conveys the gravity of what has been lost and the future she has been cruelly denied. Jealousy, pride and betrayal place even more pressure on this trio's strained circumstances. Set in an alternate reality in the 1990s, this blend of dystopian science fiction and romance raises moral questions while examining the nature of love under pressure.

As a recipient of the Nobel Prize for Literature, Ishiguro is renowned for his emotionally tense and elegiac fiction. This is one of his most widely beloved novels. It was also adapted into a film in 2010 starring Carey Mulligan, Andrew Garfield and Keira Knightley.

OPEN WATER

CALEB AZUMAH NELSON

2021

So few novels about love get the right balance between poetic feeling and poignantly rendered realistic detail. But Caleb Azumah Nelson confidently combines these elements to produce a debut that's beautifully distilled yet expansive in what it says in its story. Two young Black British people meet in a pub in South East London. Their relationship starts as a friendship and gradually eases into romance. Both are in their early–mid-twenties and trying to maintain their artistic aspirations while earning money. He's a photographer and she's a dancer.

Nelson narrates the story in the second person from the unnamed man's perspective. This gives the compelling effect of being at a distance at the same time as being privy to his innermost thoughts. It's like the act of being photographed itself, as you feel curiously both inside and outside yourself at once. The story shows that there's a freedom which accompanies intimacy, as you can truly be yourself, but there are consequences that come from such vulnerability.

This book won the Costa First Novel Award and Nelson has been hailed as one of the best new writers in Britain today.

DOCTOR THORNE

ANTHONY TROLLOPE

1858

Early on in this novel the author openly concedes that though the book's title is *Doctor Thorne*, the real hero is Frank Gresham. Frank's romantic dilemma is at the centre of this story, which continues Trollope's *Chronicles of Barsetshire* series concerning a fictional English county and its inhabitants. Frank and Doctor Thorne's niece Mary fall in love early in the novel. But Mary is an illegitimate daughter who comes from a humble background and Frank is the son of a squire who has squandered his wealth. As the only son of the Gresham household, Frank must marry for money. The drama of this couple being separated because of their different social positions plays out in a poignant way. Frank's family also try to pair him with Martha Dunstable, a wealthy heiress who realises that the men wooing her are only interested in her fortune. It's hilarious how she swats them away.

Trollope excels at creating a vibrant cast of characters whose stories play out in many funny, moving and memorable scenes. His Victorian novels are the ultimate comfort read as they are so entertaining while also giving incisive social commentary, and offer many surprising moments weighted with emotion.

STARLING DAYS

ROWAN HISAYO BUCHANAN * 2019

Mina and Oscar are a young married couple living in New York City who temporarily move to London so Oscar can help his father prepare some properties for sale. Mina struggles with deep sadness which threatens to overwhelm her and which causes her to self-harm. Her struggle with depression is depicted against Oscar's no-less heartrending emotional negligence caused by being born as an illegitimate child who seeks to forge a connection with his ageing father. Amid their struggles, Mina makes a strong romantic connection with Phoebe, an English blogger whose presence brightens Mina's world when she begins to feel overwhelmed by a suffocating loneliness. Their interactions show the challenges of building and maintaining a successful relationship while trying to manage mental health issues.

This is a beautiful tale about love, marriage and friendship. It considers the complications involved in relationships steered by dependencies that are emotional, financial and/or sexual. Buchanan portrays all her characters' journeys and dilemmas with much sympathy. Her writing has a pleasing fluidity to it in evoking all the undercurrents of emotion within her characters' lives as they navigate modern life.

SWIMMING IN THE DARK

TOMASZ JEDROWSKI

2020

Jedrowski's debut novel follows two young men over the course of the summer of 1980 in Soviet-governed Poland. Prior to starting university they meet at an agricultural camp while serving their compulsory labour requirement for the country, and embark on a passionate affair while reading James Baldwin's *Giovanni's Room*. Their relationship is described in highly romantic terms where the pair are able to discover their own paradise in a beautiful, remote, rural location. At the same time, the threat of party politics and the punishment for homosexual acts creates a tense atmosphere.

In the story Ludwik speaks directly to his lover Janusz, relating their past experiences. This adds to the heightened sense of romance as these are memories which have been retreaded in the narrator's mind until they have a smooth, hard polish. But, while the eroticism feels amplified, so does Ludwik's resentment for the disagreements which divided them. Both men realise the perilousness of their positions within the communist regime and they have differing plans on how to survive it. This very engaging story beautifully dramatises a gay romance amid a perilous time and place in history.

STAY WITH ME

AYOBAMI ADEBAYO * 2017

Yejide and Akin are an intelligent, beautiful and prosperous couple living in modern-day Nigeria. In the year 1985 it looks like they are set for a promising future, but no matter how hard the couple try, they cannot conceive a child. The narrative alternates between this couple's points of view. They convey the multi-faceted strains on their relationship as their family and society demand that they produce children. They go to extreme measures to do so and there are multiple shocking plot twists along the way. Amid the personal crisis that this couple experience, the political leadership of the country is in a precarious state, forcing them to make choices which in more stable circumstances they wouldn't have made. Although Yejide and Akin truly desire only each other, their relationship is burdened with pressures which severely test their love. It's a tragic romance that conveys the different dilemmas faced by women and men when the importance of conceiving children is placed above all else.

This debut novel received recognition from multiple book awards. Although it contains many serious themes, the story is full of such vibrant characters and fascinating surprises, it's very pleasurable to read.

MAPS FOR LOST LOVERS

NADEEM ASLAM * 2004

The lovers at the centre of this story are absent from its immediate action for reasons which become terrifyingly clear over the course of the novel. Yet, the presence of Jugnu and Chanda's passion for each other looms large in the hearts and minds of this English community, which has been renamed Dasht-e-Tanhaii by the locals who are predominantly from a Pakistani background. Between experiences of racism from outside their neighbourhood and some residents who practise a strictly orthodox form of Islam, many of the characters in this novel find their lives hemmed in by domineering ideologies which seek to restrict or punish their desires. This conflict is intensely felt between couples such as Jugnu's liberal brother Shamas and his conservative wife Kaukab. What's so striking about this novel is the delicately balanced way with which everyone's point of view is depicted. There's a great deal of compassion for each character's individuality as we come to understand the deep love they feel for one another.

Nadeem Aslam is a multi-award-winning author. Though this novel is a tragic love tale, it's also filled with hope because of the deep humanity at the heart of its story.

THE LOVE SONG OF MISS QUEENIE HENNESSY

RACHEL JOYCE * 2014

In her old age, Queenie realises that she doesn't have much time left, so she writes to Harold, the love of her life who never even knew she loved him. To her surprise, she begins receiving postcards from Harold saying that he's walking across England to visit her hospice. This provokes her to write pages and pages back to him with the assistance of one of the caring attendant nuns. Slowly the past between them is uncovered along with the complicated connection Queenie shared with Harold's son David. This is not a soft tale of love lost, but a story of raw, powerful emotion that realistically captures the things that are most joyful and excruciating about life. Yet the author also imbues the story with a tremendous sense of humour, which adds a graceful note to the vividly portrayed lives.

Rachel Joyce has described this book as a 'companion' to her debut novel *The Unlikely Pilgrimage of Harold Fry*. The two books beautifully complement each other, but this story stands on its own as all of Queenie's secrets and confessions come bursting out in her letters. It feels as if her humble past is more colourfully alive than any melodramatic tale of lost love.

MOTHERING SUNDAY

GRAHAM
SWIFT

2016

In only 132 pages this novel encapsulates a crucial day in the life of Jane Fairchild, an orphan maid at a grand country house, who eventually becomes a great writer. The day in question is Mothering Sunday, 1924. At a very elderly age, Jane looks back on what happened over the course of this day when she was still young. In beautifully stark language, Swift evokes the lingering pleasure and tension of an affair. Paul is a member of the gentry who has agreed to marry Miss Hobday, mostly for her family's money. Instead of going to meet his fiancée and her family on this day, he enjoyed an assignation with Jane. Did he want to stay with Jane instead? Was he happy to marry Miss Hobday? Or was he merely fulfilling an obligation? These questions remain suspended in the air as Jane recalls the passionate way they enjoyed each other's bodies.

What's mesmerising about this story is the way that Swift circles back to the same images and moments over and over. Memories frequently replay in Jane's mind from different angles with slight changes. It's a beautifully effective method of portraying this pivotal love affair which led her to forge a new path in life.

THE PORTABLE VEBLEN

ELIZABETH MCKENZIE * 2016

This novel is about a couple who meet and marry, but it's much more a story about families and how two people endeavour to create a life together after being raised in very different and challenging situations. Veblen is a thirty-year-old woman who lives on the remote edges of Palo Alto working secretarial temp jobs to fund her passion for translating Norwegian literature. She meets and quickly falls in love with Paul Vreeland, a thirty-five-year-old research scientist who is on the brink of discovering a revolutionary new medical treatment. They want to marry soon, but their plans are complicated by their difficult families.

Veblen's parents struggle with mental health issues. Because she's been forced into a role as their carer, she still clings to childish fantastical notions of fictional lands and talks to squirrels. Meanwhile, Paul's rebellious parents have led him to desperately seek approval from the establishment. There are many cringe-worthy tragicomic scenes as the couple meet each other's families and try to navigate how they can successfully integrate the families into the life they want to build together. It's a curious and unique book that isn't afraid to keep asking questions for which there are no easy answers.

SOPHIE AND THE SIBYL

PATRICIA DUNCKER

2015

Patricia Duncker fictionalises the final eight years of the life of author George Eliot – often referred to as 'the Sibyl' – by placing her within an intriguing love triangle. Eliot takes a shine to Max, her German publisher's ambitious younger brother. Sophie is a teenage countess and heiress to a great fortune, who plans to marry Max. However, their wedding plans are disrupted when Eliot comes between them through a series of dramatic events. Sophie is an ardent fan of Eliot's writing, but her opinion changes when Eliot intrudes upon her relationship with Max. This powerful novel shows the degrees to which our egos affect the dynamic of our relationships.

It's written in the style of a Victorian romance/Victorian comedy of manners. One of the most refreshing things about this novel is the way Patricia Duncker directly participates in it. Somehow it's as if she becomes the reader of the story alongside us, providing commentary and observations in tandem with the characters' thoughts and actions. Rather than being intrusive, this adds to the gusto of this gripping, moving and spectacular story. You don't need to be a *Middlemarch* fan to appreciate this wonderfully creative novel. It's also the most beautiful love letter to George Eliot.

MAYUMI AND THE SEA OF HAPPINESS

JENNIFER TSENG * 2015

Librarian Mayumi lives on a small island off the coast of Massachusetts with her husband Var and their young daughter Maria. Her marriage has become loveless, leaving Mayumi feeling very lonely. When a young man (whom she refuses to name throughout the novel) enters her library, he gives her the possibility of a romance that soon becomes an obsession. Mayumi has read countless novels about illicit affairs from *The Lover* to *Lolita*; she's acutely aware of the pitfalls of giving into temptation. Yet she can't resist the passion she feels for the seventeen-year-old boy she meets, making this novel a moving meditation on love in all its forms.

There are frequent references to islands throughout the book – both inhabiting a physical island and an island state of mind. Tseng brilliantly describes Mayumi's transforming state throughout the affair. This is a physical, emotional and sexual satisfaction like none she has felt in years. She knows it must eventually end, but she has been irrevocably changed. Her life becomes filled with the fear of discovery, the guilt of wronging her husband and the terror of losing this new part of her life. It's a very gripping, surprising and intimate novel. Tseng is an American writer who has published multiple poetry books.

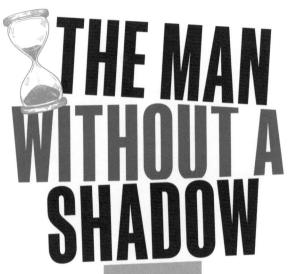

THE MAN WITHOUT A SHADOW

JOYCE
CAROL
OATES

2016

This is surely one of the most haunting love stories of all time. Elihu Hoopes experiences an inflammation of the brain in 1964, which causes him to lose all short-term memory. He is incapable of recalling anything new for more than seventy seconds. His condition is incurable and in the proceeding decades he's regularly tested at a neuroscience research facility. One of the scientists, Margot Sharpe, builds her career out of working closely with the amnesiac. The connection she forms with him turns into a strikingly original romance. Elihu's tragic condition doesn't allow him to conceptualise the future. The opposite is the case for Margot who has consciously cut herself off from her personal past. Her romantic attachment to Elihu grows even though he has no enduring awareness of her. Because she must continually introduce herself to him, she claims to be both his doctor and his wife.

Oates has a tremendous skill for immersing readers within the fluctuating emotional state of her characters. Although this is a most unusual story, it reflects how people present different versions of themselves to loved ones, and shows that even the most devoted relationships can be extinguished in a flash.

THE A TO Z OF YOU AND ME

JAMES HANNAH * 2015

Ivo is only forty years old, but he lives in a hospice due to complications of diabetes and kidney failure. He probably won't recover. In order to help distract him from this fact, a colourfully spoken and encouraging nurse named Sheila invents a game in which he has to think of a part of the body for each letter of the alphabet. In the process of doing so, Ivo has memory associations which encourage him to recall the past, deal with his guilt and mentally converse with his former girlfriend Mia. The result is a beautiful representation of one man's sadly interrupted life conveyed through fragmented memories that are both highly comic and tragic.

Ivo's condition gives him focus on what's important in life and sharpens his understanding of how he came to this point. We are cleverly led through several mysteries which are hinted at within the glimpses we're given of his past; this creates suspense, making this story a compulsive, fast read. Although this is a tragic romance and it explores many dark aspects of life, Hannah maintains a tremendous lightness of touch and skilfully depicts the complex spectrum of human emotion. The nineteenth-century medical textbook *Gray's Anatomy* partly inspired Hannah in how he structured this debut novel.

THE INCARNATIONS

SUSAN BARKER

2014

Wang is a humble cab driver in Beijing. He receives strange letters from an anonymous writer who informs him that they have known each other in several past lives. Their different incarnations are enumerated along with their shared dramatic experiences. Interspersed with these letters is an account of Wang's own troubled past and strained circumstances. He's desperate to discover who is sending these letters to him, and his present life is thrown into disorder. But he also gradually considers the possibility that this is an entangled love affair which has lasted for centuries. Tales of Wang's past lives include his experiences as a eunuch in an imperial palace in 632 CE; a crafty scarred slave named Tiger in 1213; a virginal concubine in 1542; a British cultural explorer in 1836; and a loyal Maoist of the School of Revolutionary Girls in 1966.

As well as providing snapshots of pivotal moments from China's immense history, this story allows the author to play with notions of gender, sexuality and race. A single character can flip between being a young girl in one story to a middle-aged man in another. By giving us the tales of two characters that are reincarnated continuously throughout history, Barker creates an epically romantic tale.

84, CHARING CROSS ROAD

HELENE HANFF * 1970

Before the internet, many people developed long-term relationships through written letters. American author Helene Hanff first contacted the English antiquarian booksellers Marks & Co on Charing Cross Road in 1949 because she sought obscure British literature not available in New York City. The shop's chief buyer Frank Doel responded and the two continued writing to each other over a period of twenty years. During this time they developed a wonderful friendship, which extended to Frank's wife and other staff at the bookstore. The letters they exchanged are reproduced in this book where Helene's bold attitude and Frank's shyly courteous manner stand out. Their contrasting personalities and cultures serve as the basis for many cordial exchanges through their correspondence.

This story has been adapted for TV, the stage, radio and a film starring Anne Bancroft and Anthony Hopkins. Helene and Frank never got the chance to meet in person, but their letters are a testament to a unique fraternal relationship. Although this is not a romantic love story, it's a true tale which is suffused with such powerful feelings of fond friendship and a passion for literature, it will soften the hardest of hearts.

A ROOM WITH A VIEW

E. M. FORSTER * 1908

When Lucy Honeychurch arrives at a pensione in Florence with her fussy chaperone Charlotte Bartlett, they are not given the room they were promised. They want lodging with a view of the River Arno, which leads another guest, Mr Emerson, and his son George to swap rooms with them. Though Lucy is perplexed by the behaviour of these unconventional men, she's drawn to George's passion for life. However, the more conventional gentleman Cecil Vyse seems like a much more sensible match and she eventually agrees to marry him back in England. As Lucy feels torn between the two men, she must reckon with how much she wants to adhere to convention and how much she wants to follow her heart. Forster's engrossing romantic story meaningfully illuminates how English society in the early 1900s was on the brink of change, especially for young women.

This classic novel has inspired stage and radio adaptations, as well as a 1928 hit song composed by Noël Coward. However, the most famous adaptation is the 1985 Merchant Ivory film starring Helena Bonham-Carter, Maggie Smith and Daniel Day-Lewis.

GONE WITH THE WIND

MARGARET MITCHELL

1936

Surely Scarlett O'Hara must be one of the most compelling characters in literature. Though intelligent and witty, she is thoroughly spoiled, wilful and manipulative with a tragic tendency to put off thinking about important decisions until tomorrow. She more than meets her match with cocky Rhett Butler who comes with a scandalous reputation. Their relationship plays out over the course of many years through marriages, deaths and the bloody American Civil War, which obliterates Scarlett's privileged life. In her fierce determination to survive, Scarlett must harden herself, but this also clouds her from seeing the true happiness she might find with Rhett. This is a story of truly epic proportions, which describes a young woman's transformative coming-of-age experience and one of the most monumental love affairs of all time.

This novel was a bestseller when it was first published and it was included on a list of 'Books That Shaped America' by The Library of Congress. The story was also turned into an Academy Award-winning film in which Vivien Leigh played Scarlett. However, the story also romanticises a racist caste system. Both the book and film are justly criticised for their stereotypical and derogatory portrayal of African Americans.

WOMEN IN LOVE

D. H.
LAWRENCE

1920

Though this book is a sequel to *The Rainbow*, it's considered by many to be Lawrence's finest novel. It follows the story of sisters Ursula and Gudrun Brangwen who reside in the Midlands in the 1910s. They become romantically involved with local school inspector Rupert and industrialist Gerald. As their relationship progresses, so does the complexity of their desire. All four become engaged in an intimate friendship with each other as they openly discuss issues to do with art, nature, social mobility, equality and society. However, their primary concern and romantic struggles have to do with sex and sexuality. The story forthrightly wrestles with this subject matter, but it's also about failing to become who you want to be and embracing your destiny.

A century before Sally Rooney wrote about the romantic entanglements of a group of intellectually driven individuals in early adulthood, D. H. Lawrence created similarly engaging and provocative stories. Some aspects of the books are chauvinistic, but others are surprisingly modern and progressive. Many of his novels received a limited circulation because they were too risqué for the social mores of the time, and this novel was temporarily banned in the UK.

THE WEATHER IN THE STREETS

ROSAMOND LEHMANN * 1936

What if your teenage crush suddenly appeared again later in your life? Having separated from her husband, Olivia is a single woman working as a photographer's assistant in bohemian London. One day on a train she happens to sit across from Rollo, a wealthy and privileged man she once swooned over at a ball ten years earlier. He's now married but not happily, as his wife Nicola is distant and highly strung. Though Olivia is trepidatious about getting involved with him, she can't help engaging in a heated affair. Their clandestine relationship quickly becomes consumed with hasty meetings in restaurants and sordid hotel rooms. Olivia always comes second to Nicola. Though the inevitable outcome is clear, Lehmann brilliantly captures Olivia's longing and sensitivity having become entangled in this tempestuous romance.

The novel shows how in early twentieth-century England, reputation and social standing were paramount. Olivia is driven to desperation as she can't openly express how much her illicit relationship with Rollo means to her. The honest degree to which Lehmann wrote about these issues was scandalous at the time. Though this story is a sequel to *Invitation to the Waltz*, it can be read as a stand-alone book.

ANNA KARENINA

LEO
TOLSTOY

(TRANSLATED BY
RICHARD PEVEAR
AND LARISSA
VOLOKHONSKY)

1878

Although this novel may appear daunting with its page count and enormous reputation, the passion with which Tolstoy writes about the emotions of Anna Karenina makes this story feel so fresh and alive. This is why it's considered such a timeless classic and one of the greatest novels of all time. Anna is trapped in a tedious marriage with Count Karenin. When she is romantically pursued by dashing army cavalry officer Vronsky, her world opens to the possibilities of life and love beyond the boundaries of her current circumstances. Yet leaving their homes, families and country behind to find happiness together is more challenging than the couple hope. Their passionate and tumultuous affair is at the centre of this absorbing epic, but Tolstoy also describes the journey of earnest landowner Levin's agricultural, romantic and spiritual struggles. In following the lives and fates of Tolstoy's cast of characters we're swept back to the high society of mid-nineteenth-century St Petersburg.

Given that Anna Karenina is one of the most famous characters in literature, it's no wonder that she has been portrayed by some of the greatest actresses, including Greta Garbo, Vivien Leigh, Jacqueline Bisset and Keira Knightley.

THE GRADUATE

CHARLES WEBB * 1963

While it might seem like the stereotype that middle-aged men have affairs with younger women, the reverse can certainly also be true. In this novella, Benjamin Braddock returns to his family's suburban home in California having recently graduated from college. He feels uncertain about what direction he wants his life to take. Mrs Robinson is the wife of his father's business partner, stuck in a marriage which she characterises as loveless. She overtly seduces wayward Benjamin who eventually capitulates. Although Benjamin subsequently falls in love with Mrs Robinson's daughter Elaine, the jealous mother is furious at the prospect of Elaine being with her one-time lover. This is a scandalous story of sexual awakening and flying in the face of convention.

Because Charles Webb wrote this novella shortly after graduating from college, it has long been assumed that it is partly autobiographical, but the author never admitted this. However, he did live an uncommon lifestyle, relinquishing most of his family's wealth and substantial royalties that he could have earned from the famous film version of the book. *The Graduate*, starring Anne Bancroft and Dustin Hoffman, is deemed one of the greatest American films of all time.

DOCTOR ZHIVAGO

BORIS PASTERNAK
(TRANSLATED BY RICHARD PEVEAR
AND LARISSA VOLOKHONSKY)

1957

Yury Zhivago is a poet and philosopher as well as a physician. Amid being swept into the brutality and confusion of the Russian Civil War, he finds himself torn between two women. There is Yury's loving wife Tonya and there is his lover Lara who has a husband of her own. In addition to being his passionate companions, these women serve as muses to Yury as he persists in writing poems through deprivation and harsh winters spent in exile. The dramatic circumstances of this rapidly transforming society alternately tear these characters apart and bring them back together over a long period of time. Pasternak atmospherically evokes a sense of high adventure with train journeys through Russia's snowy landscape that lead to heartrending encounters. The large cast of characters can be confusing, but this is an epic story worth persisting with – it's utterly original and richly rewarding.

Doctor Zhivago could initially be read only outside of Pasternak's native country, as it was refused publication in the USSR, and he declined the Nobel Prize in Literature under pressure from the KGB. However, it has now been incorporated into the Russian school curriculum.

MADAME BOVARY

GUSTAVE FLAUBERT * 1856
(TRANSLATED BY ADAM THORPE)

When naive provincial girl Emma Rouault finds herself being courted by the area's amicable local doctor, she eagerly accepts his offer of marriage. She believes that such a partnership will grant her entry to a world of luxury and romance that she has thus far only read about in novels. What a disappointment to discover that her husband Charles Bovary is a colossal bore! Neither motherhood nor trips to the opera appease her yearning for art, adventure and passion, so Emma finds companionship with different handsome gentlemen. However, she doesn't anticipate the perils which accompany such affairs. Flaubert depicts Emma's plight with dignity and respect. Her realistically portrayed tale reveals all our inner desires, fears, frustrations and unrealised dreams.

When this story first appeared in serialised form, public prosecutors derided the novel. Flaubert was charged in court with having committed an outrage to public morality and religion. He was soon acquitted, and the publicity which resulted from the scandal contributed to the book becoming a bestseller. It's an established classic that is enthralling to read and whose tragic romance deepens in meaning from being reread.

THE
NARROWS

ANN
PETRY

1953

This novel takes place in a neighbourhood within the fictional town of Monmouth, Connecticut. A section of this community which is largely populated by African Americans is nicknamed 'The Narrows'. When dashing and highly educated Link Williams helps a white woman who calls herself Camilo avoid an altercation, he takes her to a local bar and an attraction blooms between them. They have an affair, which grows increasingly passionate until Link discovers that Camilo is concealing her true identity – she is married and wealthy.

The narrative is skilfully written as it moves from the present to a series of poignant flashbacks. Given the social stigmas and prejudice of the time, an interracial romance that's set in mid-twentieth-century America is bound to be accompanied by harrowing difficulties. There is a lot of betrayal, deceit and shocking drama within this story. But it also includes a great deal of beauty, deft humour and subtle meaning. Some scenes also positively erupt with passion.

Ann Petry was a pioneering author whose powerful writing regarding racism included journalism as well as bestselling fiction. Her work has recently experienced a revival.

THINGS WE NEVER SAID

NICK ALEXANDER * 2017

Sean and Catherine built a long and productive life together. From the birth of their daughter April to professional triumphs and disappointments, they made a strong partnership. However, Catherine just lost her battle with cancer, leaving Sean a widower with nothing but his memories of their marriage. The book opens with her funeral. At her wake Sean is given a simply wrapped cardboard box by a trusted friend. It's a final gift from Catherine that holds a series of numbered envelopes, each containing a photograph and a cassette tape. Catherine documented her memories of the event depicted in the pictures, each of which represents a different milestone in their relationship. Sean is surprised to discover that her perspective on certain things they experienced together can sometimes dramatically differ from how he recalls them, leaving him with an entirely new understanding of his wife and the love they shared.

While this might seem like a melancholy premise for a novel, it's a story filled with joy and humour as well as sorrow. There are also some surprises and revelations. It creatively probes the question of how well you can ever really know the person you love – especially if you've shared an entire life together.

TIPPING THE VELVET

SARAH WATERS * 1998

In 1890s England Nancy 'Nan' Astley grows up among a working-class family in Kent, shucking oysters and preparing seafood for her family's business. She longs for something much more than this rural life, but doesn't know what she's looking for – until she meets Kitty who is a 'masher', or male impersonator performing at a local theatre. The two strike up a friendship so that when Kitty leaves for London, Nan leaps at the opportunity to accompany this vivacious woman as her dresser. The bustling city opens up an enormous range of experiences and opportunities. Not only does Nan discover she has a knack for performance herself, but also she realises that she possesses a strong sexual desire for Kitty. She encounters betrayal, heartache and misadventure in this city filled with colourful characters and historical curiosities. This is a sumptuous tale that's a journey of self-discovery as much as it is about finding someone to truly love.

Sarah Waters burst onto the literary scene with this debut, leading some critics to wonder if she'd invented a new genre of the lesbian picaresque novel. It's a riveting story of romantic strife, but also gives a new view of different levels of late-Victorian English life.

THE
PRICE
OF
SALT

PATRICIA HIGHSMITH

1952

Though Therese seems to be making a promising start in life working at a Manhattan department store and dating a steady man, she often feels lonely and dissatisfied. One day an elegant and striking woman named Carol enters her section of the store and gives Therese her address so that her purchases may be delivered. The two strike up a friendship and their relationship eventually develops into a beautiful romance. But Carol is fearful of continuing the affair because she's going through a divorce with her husband, which includes a custody battle for their child. The story is filled with romantic tension as two women try to maintain a loving relationship amid the prejudices of the time.

This novel is not only notable for its sympathetic portrayal of a same-sex couple, but it offers a relatively happy ending, which was very unusual for lesbian literature of this era. Patricia Highsmith originally published the book under a pseudonym because of its explicit lesbian content and because the story was so personal to her. She eventually admitted ownership of the novel and it was republished as *Carol*. It was also adapted into an exquisite film using the alternative title, starring Cate Blanchett and Rooney Mara.

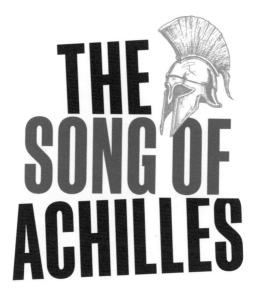

THE SONG OF ACHILLES

MADELINE MILLER * 2011

Teenage romance is often difficult enough to manage without being burdened by prophesies, warring kingdoms and the wrath of Greek gods. When sensitive Patroclus, the son of King Menoetius, is exiled after a fatal accident, he meets the dashing and talented Achilles. A strong friendship gradually develops into a passionate romance while the pair receive expert training from a wise centaur. Not even Achilles' overprotective sea nymph mother Thetis can keep the two apart. But Achilles is called to a larger cause and both young men are drawn into Agamemnon's extended bloody military campaign against Troy. Patroclus must watch in despair as the love of his life fulfils his destiny and transforms into a figure of legend. Miller gives an entirely new view of Homer's *Iliad* by immersing us in the perspective of Achilles' loyal male lover. It's a beautifully emotional story which is truly epic.

Even if you don't know anything about Greek myths, this novel is thoroughly immersive and relatable. It won the Orange Prize for Fiction (now known as the Women's Prize for Fiction) and later became a social-media favourite after TikTok videos about the book went viral. Miller inventively shows that there's much more to the saga of Achilles than his dodgy heel.

DAYS WITHOUT END

SEBASTIAN BARRY * 2016

The battlefields of the American Indian Wars and American Civil War might not seem like spaces where romance would be found, but this novel describes a uniquely hopeful love story. Thomas McNulty escapes the Irish famine to become a soldier in nineteenth-century America where he meets another handsome soldier named John Cole. They develop a strong emotional and sexual connection amid many bloody battles. They fight in these wars not for ideological reasons but because of economic necessity. While the meaning of these conflicts remains ambiguous for Thomas, the way he and John feel about each other is certain.

In addition to being an innovative war romance, the story gives a fascinating perspective on gender and sexuality. At one point Thomas and John join a cabaret where they entertain audiences of men while dressed in drag. There's a kind of liberation in this, as they aren't constricted by traditional masculinity. It also provides crucial training for Thomas when later he must disguise himself as a woman.

This novel won the Costa Book of the Year Award and is part of a group of novels Barry has written about the McNulty clan.

TIN MAN

SARAH WINMAN

2017

DATE READ

A complex love triangle is at the centre of this melancholy novel about art and romance. When we first meet Ellis he's a middle-aged widower who diligently works at a factory and sifts through photographs from the past. His dream of becoming a painter has faded. He recalls long cycle rides with his childhood friend Michael and, later, an idyllic trip they took to the south of France. Ellis also has fond memories of the period of time when he, Michael and Ellis' wife Annie formed a close friendship. But that abruptly ended and he has now been left alone. The reasons for this are gradually revealed as the narrative switches to Michael's perspective. Between missed opportunities and chance circumstances, these individuals are painfully aware that their lives might have turned out so differently.

Though this is a novel suffused with sorrow and an aching sense of nostalgia, Winman writes with a powerful precision that conveys how finding true love is worth any heartbreak. Each page is filled with the intensity of these characters' passion for beauty and romance. It's a story that gives a new perspective on freedom, solitude and the impact we make upon each other's lives.

THE AGE OF INNOCENCE

EDITH WHARTON * 1920

There's a nostalgic tinge to this breathtakingly romantic story set amongst the upper classes of 1870s New York City. Written after the First World War, it's a portrait of a society that Wharton was very aware had permanently vanished. This adds an emotional undercurrent to the tale of Newland Archer, a gentleman lawyer whose future seems fully laid out as he's engaged to the beautiful and proper May Welland. But when May's cousin, the free-spirited Ellen Olenska, arrives, Newland develops a passion for her which he struggles to control, and questions if he must continue to follow this society's strict customs. Wealth and appearances are of vital importance; those that lose their respectability are closed out.

What makes this story especially engaging is the author's portrayal of deeply embedded conventions and dynamic characterisations. For instance, though May initially appears simple, she possesses strategic plans to keep her husband and maintain their social standing. The novel questions the meaning of innocence on many different levels. It won the Pulitzer Prize for Fiction. Wharton was the first woman to obtain this award, which cemented her place as one of the leading American writers of the twentieth century.

POSSESSION

A. S.
BYATT

1990

While doing research in the London Library, academic Roland Mitchell discovers old handwritten drafts of a romantic letter by Randolph Ash, a fictional Victorian poet of prominence. When Mitchell realises this letter isn't addressed to Ash's wife, he knows he's on the brink of making a shocking biographical discovery which could make his career. Not only was Ash's amorous missive written for a woman he was having an affair with, but that woman turns out to be Christabel LaMotte, another respected poet of the time. Mitchell teams up with a LaMotte scholar named Maud Bailey to uncover more clues about this clandestine affair. A beautiful historical romance unfolds alongside the stories of the academics' romance. What they unearth turns out to have more personal significance for them than they ever imagined.

Byatt convincingly invents the lives of two poets by combining elements of narrative, diary entries, letters and poetry, which also serve as pieces to a romantic mystery. Not only does the story evocatively describe secret love affairs, but the way the author describes time spent with great literature has a romantically charged quality to it. This novel won the Booker Prize, and it was turned into a film starring Gwyneth Paltrow.

LOVE IN THE TIME OF CHOLERA

GABRIEL GARCÍA MÁRQUEZ * 1985
(TRANSLATED BY EDITH GROSSMAN)

Can romantic obsession be trusted? Florentino and Fermina are lovestruck youths who carefully try to keep their relationship a secret from her domineering father. When he discovers they've been meeting, he tears them apart. But Fermina gradually realises on her own that their passion was a product of teenage dreams and marries the eminent Dr Urbino, a national hero committed to eradicating cholera. Although Florentino knows he can't compete with her husband and he engages in many more affairs, he continues to believe that Fermina is the true love of his life. The story scrutinises both volatile affairs and steady marriages to question the real meaning of romance.

One of this Nobel-Prize-winning author's great powers was his ability to depict sensuality in epic terms without melodrama. This novel dramatises passion and faithfulness through the experiences of relationships, marriage and old age. Its setting in a port city near the Caribbean Sea beautifully evokes a romantically charged atmosphere. However, there's also the unsettling knowledge of a disease which perniciously spreads like doubt within a love affair. It's touching that Márquez based the early part of this couple's story on his parents' lives.

THIS
MUST BE
THE PLACE

MAGGIE O'FARRELL

2016

Claudette walks away from her famous director husband and a successful acting career to live in a remote Irish retreat with her new husband Daniel. However, Daniel has children from his first marriage, an unresolved secret and a growing substance-abuse problem. Each chapter focuses on a specific character related to this couple. These include Daniel's son Niall who struggles with a severe eczema condition and Claudette's sister-in-law Maeve who journeys to China to adopt a daughter. These individual stories leap back and forth through time to give impressions of Daniel and Claudette's tumultuous relationship. The cumulative effect is a kaleidoscopic portrait of the way chance and coincidence influence the most important decisions of our lives.

O'Farrell realistically portrays the quirks, humour and heartache of family life. She also beautifully describes how those who love us see us in an idealistic light, which in turn reinforces our own self-confidence. This novel meaningfully shows how complex relationships can be and that we inevitably follow lots of indirect paths in life, but also how powerfully changed we can become when honest connections are made.

MAURICE

E. M. FORSTER * 1971

Inspired by ancient-Greek writings about same-sex love, Maurice Hall develops a romantic relationship with fellow student Clive Durham while they are studying at Cambridge. After university, Clive marries a woman and Maurice endeavours to suppress his homosexual nature by seeing a hypnotist. But, when Maurice has an intense sexual encounter with working-class Alec at the Durhams' estate, he can't deny he wants to pursue a full relationship with this labourer. Conflict between them forms because of the illicit nature of their love and their class differences. This tender love story gives a fascinating glimpse of a bygone age while also providing a hopeful message that true romance can overcome any social barrier.

Although E. M. Forster was famous for his series of novels dissecting class difference and hypocrisy in English society, he didn't openly publish any fiction concerning homosexuality in his lifetime. He originally wrote the manuscript for *Maurice* in 1913–14, but it didn't appear in print until several months after his death; Forster was familiar with the way literature which radically challenged social mores was prosecuted. It's a moving book and a valuable testament of forbidden love.

THE SNOW BALL

BRIGID BROPHY

1964

A New Year's Eve masquerade ball held in a grand Georgian mansion makes an ideal setting for romance and mischief. A feverish excitement builds during this glamorous party as the music swells, the hall fills with laughter and a light snowfall settles outside. There's a mood of magic as the guests dance, gossip and flirt deep into the night. Anna arrives disguised as the Commendatore's daughter Donna Anna from Mozart's opera. Therefore it seems like fate when she's met on the dance floor by a darkly cloaked figure masked as the seducer Don Giovanni. They kiss and Anna is filled with passion, but does she want to know who this man really is, or to maintain the excitement of mystery?

We follow this pair and two other couples over the course of several hours as they steal away for assignations or gaze upon others from a distance. The thrill of the party builds, but everyone is mindful that the dawn will eventually come and the guests must again face the cold light of reality. Brophy brilliantly plays with how we allow ourselves to be romanced and the ways that we can slip out of the shackles of identity to become someone new.

A LONG PETAL OF THE SEA

ISABEL ALLENDE * 2019
(TRANSLATED BY NICK CAISTOR
AND AMANDA HOPKINSON)

Two individuals have their promising futures derailed by a tumultuous revolution and discover a loving relationship that they never anticipated. Roser is a talented musician who comes from an impoverished background. She falls in love with tough militiaman Guillem who is drawn into fighting in the Spanish Civil War. When he is lost in battle and the brutal Franco regime comes into power, Roser must flee the country while heavily pregnant. Guillem's brother Victor was training to be a doctor when the war erupted and assists Roser's escape. The Chilean government provided asylum for Spanish refugees under a scheme devised by the poet Pablo Neruda. Victor finds a way for him and Roser to start a new life for themselves in South America, but in order to be granted entry, they must marry each other.

This dramatic and riveting novel shows how a deep love can grow out of a partnership created in desperate times. As it follows the turbulent political changes occurring in two different countries, it also movingly demonstrates the way personal transformation leads to a series of passionate affairs. Allende has received many awards and is renowned as one of the world's most widely read Spanish-language authors.

PRIDE AND PREJUDICE

JANE AUSTEN * 1813

Has there been a more disastrous first meeting between potential lovers than that of Miss Elizabeth Bennet and Mr Darcy? Nobody could blame this witty young woman for becoming instantly prejudiced against this proud and wealthy man who refuses to dance with her at a ball. However, the intellectual sparring match between this pair develops into a simmering romance filled with intrigue, surprising revelations and comedy. Both of these lively, stubborn characters must overcome their own faults to truly connect and understand one another. Though one of the Bennet daughters must marry for money, Elizabeth is determined to make a match with more depth of feeling. But what if she could enter into a marriage that includes love and financial security?

Austen's classic Regency-set novel of manners has been captivating readers since its publication, making it one of the most popular books in English literature. It has led to numerous film and TV adaptations, but which actor best played the aloof heart-throb Mr Darcy – Laurence Olivier, Colin Firth or Matthew Macfadyen? Whatever your preference, this story continues to inspire readers as these headstrong characters bicker and follow a circuitous pathway to romance.

FAVOURITE READS

★ _____

★ _____

★ _____

★ _____

★ _____

★ _____

★ _____

★ _____

★ _____

★ _____

★ _____

★ _____

★ _____

★ _____

★ _____

★ _____

★ _____

★ _____

TBR PILE

★ _____

★ _____

★ _____

★ _____

★ _____

★ _____

★ _____

★ _____

★ _____

★ _____

★ _____

★ _____

★ _____

★ _____

★ _____

★ _____

★ _____

★ _____

_____

THOUGHTS

INDEX

84, Charing Cross Road 56–7

A

A Long Petal of the Sea 100–1
A Room With a View 58–9
The A to Z of You and Me 52–3
Aciman, André 14–15
Adebayo, Ayobami 36–7
Adichie, Chimamanda Ngozi 20–1
The Age of Innocence 88–9
Alexander, Nick 76–7
Allende, Isabel 100–1
Americanah 20–1
Anna Karenina 66–7
Aslam, Nadeem 38–9
Austen, Jane 102–3

B

Barker, Susan 54–5
Barry, Sebastian 84–5
Bridget Jones's Diary 8–9
Brontë, Emily 6–7
Brooklyn 24–5
Brophy, Brigid 98–9
Buchanan, Rowan Hisayo 32–3
Byatt, A.S. 90–1

C

Call me by Your Name 14–15

D

Days Without End 84–5
Doctor Thorne 30–1
Doctor Zhivago 70–1

Du Maurier, Daphne 18–19
Duncker, Patricia 46–7

F

Fielding, Helen 8–9
Flaubert, Gustave 72–3
Forster, E.M. 58–9, 96–7

G

García Márquez, Gabriel 92–3
Gone with the Wind 60–1
The Graduate 68–9

H

Hall, Radclyffe 16–17
Hanff, Helene 56–7
Hannah, James 52–3
Highsmith, Patricia 80–1

I

The Incarnations 54–5
Ishiguro, Kazuo 26–7

J

Jedrowski, Tomasz 34–5
Joyce, Rachel 40–1

L

Lawrence, D.H. 62–3
Lehmann, Rosamond 64–5
Love in the Time of Cholera 92–3
The Love Song of Miss Queenie Hennessy 40–1

M

Madame Bovary 72–3
The Man Without a Shadow 50–1
Maps for Lost Lovers 38–9
Maurice 96–7
Mayumi and the Sea of Happiness 48–9
McKenzie, Elizabeth 44–5
The Mermaid of Black Conch 22–3
Miller, Madeline 82–3
Mitchell, Margaret 60–1
Mothering Sunday 42–3

N

The Narrows 74–5
Nelson, Caleb Azumah 28–9
Never Let Me Go 26–7
Nicholls, David 4–5
Niffenegger, Audrey 10–11
Normal People 12–13

O

Oates, Joyce Carol 50–1
O'Farrell, Maggie 94–5
One Day 4–5
Open Water 28–9

P

Pasternak, Boris 70–1
Petry, Ann 74–5
The Portable Veblen 44–5
Possession 90–1
The Price of Salt 80–1
Pride and Prejudice 102–3

R

Rebecca 18–19
Roffey, Monique 22–3
Rooney, Sally 12–13

S

The Snow Ball 98–9
The Song of Achilles 82–3
Sophie and the Sybil 46–7
Starling Days 32–3
Stay With Me 36–7
Swift, Graham 42–3
Swimming in the Dark 34–5

T

Things We Never Said 76–7
This Must be the Place 94–5
The Time Traveler's Wife 10–11
Tin Man 86–7
Tipping the Velvet 78–9
Tóibín, Colm 24–5
Tolstoy, Leo 66–7
Trollope, Anthony 30–1
Tseng, Jennifer 48–9

W

Waters, Sarah 78–9
The Weather in the Streets 64–5
Webb, Charles 68–9
The Well of Loneliness 16–17
Wharton, Edith 88–9
Winman, Sarah 86–7
Women in Love 62–3
Wuthering Heights 6–7

Published in 2022 by Murdoch Books, an imprint of Allen & Unwin

Murdoch Books UK
Ormond House
26–27 Boswell Street
London WC1N 3JZ
Phone: +44 (0) 20 8785 5995
murdochbooks.co.uk
info@murdochbooks.co.uk

Murdoch Books Australia
83 Alexander Street
Crows Nest NSW 2065
Phone: +61 (0)2 8425 0100
murdochbooks.com.au
info@murdochbooks.com.au

For corporate orders and custom publishing, contact our business
development team at salesenquiries@murdochbooks.com.au

Publisher: Céline Hughes
Designer: Madeleine Kane
Production Director: Niccolò De Bianchi

ISBN 978 1 92261 646 3

A catalogue record for this book is available from the British Library

A catalogue record for this
book is available from the
National Library of Australia

Colour reproduction by Born Group, London, UK
Printed by Print Best, Estonia

10 9 8 7 6 5 4 3 2 1

MIX
Paper from
responsible sources
FSC® C129413